Published By Adam Gilbin

@ Kent Chill

Money Mastery: Steps to a Money-minded Life

and Financial Success

All Right RESERVED

ISBN 978-87-94477-69-7

TABLE OF CONTENTS

Chapter 1 1

The Money Mindset 1

Chapter 2 26

Attract More Wealth With Positive Affirmation . 26

Chapter 3 31

How To Develop A Financially Positive Attitude? 31

Chapter 4 34

How To Change Your Perception Of Money And Attract Wealth 34

Chapter 5 39

Affirmations To Attract Money And Grow Your Wealth 39

Chapter 6 46

Introduction To The Poverty Mindset: Awakening The Mind 46

Chapter 7 51

The Power Of Mindfulness And Awakening The Mind 51

Chapter 8 70

Understanding Your Money Story 70

Chapter 9 78

Mindset Magic—Paving The Way To Financial Prosperity 78

Chapter 10 84

Online Business And Money-Making 84

Chapter 11 113

The Laws Of Attraction 113

Chapter 12	120
Receiving Money	120
Chapter 13	128
Expanding Your Income Streams	128
Chapter 14	138
Leveraging Your Skills And Talents	138

Chapter 1

The Money Mindset

Money is always an important topic in the modern economy, since we all deal with it every day. For many people, money constitutes the main value measure and is a universal equivalent; money can be exchanged for any product, work, service, or intangible good; they are used as an intermediary that makes the process of market exchange more convenient and accessible.

Now, even a common man knows that money is just a quantity of paper with certain properties. However, three hundred years ago, the world was a very different place. No one had heard of paper money, so it had no value.

Prosperity is important. In fact, we are well aware of this. However, we all approach them in our own unique ways. Someone will do anything for money, while for another person financial stability is not a top priority. Moreover, such people do not face economic difficulties. What gives?

Money can be viewed in different ways by different people, but if it suddenly disappears or appears, it has a profound effect on the human psyche. Some people become so financially stressed that they resort to illegal activities such as gambling or theft. However, the importance of money in today's world cannot be denied. It is essential for those who want to create a successful life for themselves and their family. In addition, financial resources facilitate individual growth and creative expression, although the extent to which this is accomplished ultimately depends on the individual.

In today's world, money plays an important role in the functioning of any business. Cash is the most liquid form of working capital. Cash is used to settle all transactions for delivery of tangible assets and performance of services. The latter can be of monetary or non-monetary nature. The state should act swiftly to increase the flow of both physical cash and electronic payments to reduce inflation and improve efficiency.

Having considered the relevance of the topic, it is possible to formulate the purpose and objectives of the work.

The goal of the research was to shed light on the function and significance of money in our lives. I have identified the following tasks for the work in accordance with the goal:

- *Assess* the value of money in the contemporary world;
- *Conduct* a survey to determine how important money is to city dwellers. *Take* into account the nature and origin of money;
- *Describe* the purposes and varieties of currency;

Making a lot of money requires a lot of motivation. However, it's crucial to cultivate the proper attitude toward money and avoid becoming reliant on its abundance. Wealth belongs to those who are skilled with money, can set priorities, manage cash flow, and keep costs under control.

Money plays a significant role in our lives. It is a tool that can be used to achieve our goals, provide for our needs, and improve our quality of life. but it's important to keep in mind that money is not the only thing that matters. There are many other things that contribute to our happiness and well-being, such as our relationships, our health, and our sense of purpose.

Here are some of the ways that money can impact our lives:

Money can help us meet our basic needs. This includes food, shelter, clothing, and healthcare. Without money, it can be difficult to meet these basic needs, which can lead to stress, anxiety, and even illness.

Money can help us achieve our goals. Whether it is buying a house, starting a business, or travelling the world, money can make it possible to achieve our goals. It can also give us the freedom to choose the kind of life we want to live.

Money can help us improve our quality of life. Money can be used to buy things that make our lives more comfortable and enjoyable, such as a nice home, a reliable car, or a vacation. It can also be used to invest in our education, our health, and our retirement.

Money isn't everything, though. There are many other things that contribute to our happiness and well-being, such as our relationships, our health, and our sense of purpose. If we focus too much on money, we may miss out on the things that are truly important in life.

Here are some tips for understanding the role of money in your life:

Set financial goals. What do you want to achieve with your money? Do you want to start a business, save for retirement, or buy a house? Making a plan to achieve your objectives can be done once you are aware of what you want to accomplish.

Create a budget. A plan for how you intend to spend your money is what's known as a budget. It can assist you in keeping track of your expenditures and ensuring that you are not spending more than necessary.

Live below your means. This means you should spend less than you earn. This can help you save money and get a better handle on your finances.

Invest your money. Investing can increase your wealth. There are many different ways to invest your money, so you can choose an option that is right for you.

Get help if you need it. If you are struggling to manage your money, there are many resources available to help you. You can get financial advice, enrol in a financial literacy course, or join a support group.

Money can improve our lives. However, it is important to use it wisely and to remember that it is not the only thing that matters in life.

Money thinking: why don't those who are afraid to spend money have money?

We often feel awkward when we talk about money, whether we're asking for a raise, bargaining for a discount, lending money, or charging a price for our services. When there is not enough money, we hate to admit it, on the other hand, we despise them for being dependent on them, and they are given to us with difficulty. There are many confusing contradictions associated with money in our minds. We are afraid of money because "money ruins people" and we want to be loved. We refuse money because it is considered noble, spiritual, good. And if we want money, then we think of ourselves as a selfish, callous person.

At the same time, being poor is not cool. We buy things and attributes that show our status.

How to figure it out?

Money is an indicator of your condition, it shows how you think, how you treat yourself and others, how you perceive the world and whether you manage your own life. These are the thoughts and beliefs that affect how you earn money, how you store it, and how you manage it.

Therefore, if you understand that you do not have enough money and this makes you anxious and sad, you should figure out what you really think about money.

We can say that there is adult and child thinking. A person with adult thinking will always have money - even in a difficult situation, he will find a way to earn money. And vice versa, a person with a childish attitude, even earning decent money, is unlikely to be able to have serious savings and manage them.

What's with the subconscious?

We know intellectually what needs to be done, but the subconscious mind can make us do things differently. For example, if your parents said something similar to "we have never been rich - there is nothing to start", then you may notice that your money seems to be slipping through your fingers, you spend everything you earn, deny yourself a lot and you never get what you want. In other words, you know that you can do more, but in your subconscious there is a belief that you are not worthy of it.

Or if your parents worked hard and returned home exhausted, then you may have a mental template that work is a place where you do not what you want, but get paid for it, and everyone lives like that. And it will be very difficult for you to imagine that work can be called a life's work, which can be pleasant and exciting and at the same time very well paid.

Having heard advice from friends to work more in order to earn more, see if they themselves have become wealthy? On the contrary, people who build their lives around joy and creativity, rather than around work, are more likely to succeed.

If you are striving for financial well-being, then the shortest way to it is to restructure your thinking.

Our immediate environment has an equally strong influence on us: if among your friends it is customary to believe that big money is given only by hard work, takes most of your life, requires sacrificing health or moral principles, then most likely your income will grow very slowly , and not you, but your colleague will receive a promotion.

We do not want to be outcasts, our fear of ostracism (fear of being expelled) and the subconscious mind will resist in every possible way exiting the system. Just like our brain.

What does your brain think about money?

The main task of our brain is to ensure our survival, not to make us rich and prosperous. The brain began to form millions of years ago, and its main task was to save us from predators, help get food, and adapt to environmental changes. Two departments were responsible for this: the reptilian brain - our instincts - and the limbic system, which provides an adequate emotional response to stimuli.

But today we are forced to solve the problems of the 21st century, and this requires other mechanisms: development, change, learning something new. This creates an internal conflict, because the brain as a whole does not like change, it strives for predictability and optimization of processes. Notice how difficult it is for us to build new habits into our lives and how much effort it takes.

The good news is that if we were previously told that nerve cells do not regenerate, now it is scientifically proven that they do just that. And as soon as we begin to tune the brain to change, nerve cells begin to create new neural connections. This process is called neuroplasticity.

In other words, if you are striving for financial well-being, then the shortest path to it is to restructure your thinking.

How to set up cash flow?

We all consider ourselves smart and educated people, but when we look at those who earn many times more, even without, in our opinion, outstanding abilities, we have the question "what is wrong with us?

It's the same with us. Not so with what and how we think, and there are three main points that affect this.

How we perceive ourselves who we are, what we are and where we belong.

Understanding how the world we live in works.

Strategies that we use in everyday life.

Attitude towards yourself is the foundation of this construction, because how much you earn directly depends on who you consider yourself and how you feel about yourself.

If you consider yourself an unworthy person, a loser who has everything in the past, a lazy person or an impostor, you will not earn big money. After all, we always get as much as we value ourselves.

Test yourself by answering the following questions:

Do you constantly compare yourself to others and often lose in your own eyes?

Do you react sharply to criticism, take everything seriously?

Do you value other people's opinions more, and is it difficult for you to make decisions without consulting?

Are you trying not to take responsibility?

Do you tend to appreciate what you do and find it hard to accept praise?

Do you identify with your results: if everything worked out, are you a hero, if not, a miserable loser?

Are you more likely to do what you should but not what you want?

If you agree with at least some of the statements, then you should work on developing your own value. Because in essence you are the most important person in your life, the one in whom you should invest, who you should take care of, support and protect in the first place. Your quality of life and financial well-being directly depend on how you feel about yourself, who you see yourself and how you manifest yourself.

About the system we live in

We all have different ideas about the world in which we live, but no matter what, natural processes remain the same. Every living being on the planet has its own mission - it is to be born, become as big and strong as possible, and begin to flourish: to interact with the outside world, developing and multiplying. And when this mission is completed, we return to the earth and become elements of a new life.

Everything is part of the system: we must grow up with all available resources, learn to do what we do best, start to communicate with other people and contribute to the world. Our mission is to create.

The same applies to money: you cannot grow, prosper and develop without such an important resource as money. You need money to invest in yourself, increase your opportunities and help others.

Therefore, the idea of living modestly and being content with little is against the system. How can you help people if you yourself need money? How will you benefit the world and create if you only think about how to make ends meet?

How to stop needing?

It is worth noting that in our country the mentioned stereotypes of thinking are strong, because neither our parents, nor our grandmothers or great-grandmothers had a lot of money. And what they instilled in us - to be part of the crowd, not to draw attention to yourself - was a sure way to survive. But times have changed, there is no need to survive anymore. To make good money, you need to be visible and make yourself known, now the value of individuality, personality with charisma.

Many people think that our world is like communicating vessels, and if there is an increase somewhere, then somewhere it will decrease. That money can run out, stop coming, their flow can dry up forever. Therefore, they save for a rainy day, save, do not buy anything for themselves, scold themselves if they spent more than planned.

You do not think that you will suddenly forget how to breathe or walk? Or that the sun won't rise tomorrow? There will always be money.

If you say to yourself well, nothing, others somehow live on this money, or "we have enough, or you can't get everything at once" - these are templates. Looking forward to a black day? He will surely come. Are you afraid that someone will come and take your earnings from you? Someday circumstances will be such that this will happen.

Such thoughts form a state of need and dissatisfaction.

And no matter how much you earn, this happens to people with a wide variety of income levels.

About strategies

Many people think that if they earn more, they will feel better, but this is not a fact. Because the style of redistributing your income will be the same. The higher you grow in money, the more tasks you have to solve - it's like moving to a new level. And if you drag your old self into new circumstances, you will be unhappy. When your income grows, you need new knowledge about saving and increasing, and just keeping a budget is no longer enough: what's the point of looking at the numbers and spending the same amount.

Usually people just start investing in improving the quality of life: changing cars, apartments, clothes, spending money on more expensive services and pleasures. And this leads to the fact that as your income grows, expenses begin to grow even faster. And you don't get rich, you get poorer.

You need to create capital, a financial reserve - to increase the difference between income and expenses. The more income you have, the more stable you are.

When your income grows, you need new knowledge about saving and increasing, just keeping a budget is no longer enough.

It is equally important to close debts and loans. Don't spend what you haven't earned yet.

You also need to think about your safety, because the concern for maintaining and increasing your new income and acquisitions increases anxiety and anxiety. Insure your life, your property and health. Then, under unforeseen circumstances, insurance payments will cover everything, and you will not have to take money out of your own wallet.

Invest. Money has to work. Now there are many brokers on the market who can tell you how to make money slowly but surely, there are many courses on financial well-being. Or find a mentor you trust.

But the most reliable investments are investments in yourself, in your development and education. The more you invest in yourself, the greater the return.

The same principle is true for all investments: the more you limit yourself and save, the less comes to you. Money is not in vain associated with energy, the more valuable what you give, the more you get back, it's like inhaling and exhaling. To receive, you must give.

As soon as you think about how you want to live in 10 years, the concern for financial well-being will come to the fore. Therefore, the faster you start working on your relationship with money, thinking and doing things that you have never done before, the faster you will achieve outstanding results.

Chapter 2

Attract More Wealth With Positive Affirmation

Affirmations may help you attract riches, and they are really easy. Financial success begins in the mind.

You may learn how to attract money more readily if you have a positive attitude toward money, enjoy reading about it, and know how to manage it well.

However, if you have unfavorable beliefs about money, such as the notions that it's difficult to get, that you'll never have enough of it, or that you detest checking your bank account because you're terrified of what it could reveal, guess what?

It will be extremely tough for you to earn, save, and handle your finances.

Furthermore, it's unlikely that you will ever reach a point where you are completely worry-free about money.

The good news is that you can alter your mindset about money and draw riches by using straightforward, practical affirmations every day.

Why It Seems Unsettling to Attract Wealth

Early signals we hear about money shape our early perceptions of it. Check to see if any of these situations seem familiar to you.

We learn that money doesn't make people happy when we hear our parents fighting about what they don't have.

When we are informed that the great gadget we truly want is too costly, we interpret this as evidence that we are undeserving of the good things that money can provide.

We know that handling our finances is tedious and challenging when we hear grownups complaining about filing their taxes.

Regardless of the event, we develop unfavorable attitudes toward money that undermine our ability to succeed financially.

Let's examine some of the misconceptions that surround bringing success into your life in more detail and see if any of these ideas align with your personal views.

Earning Wealth Would Be Against the Family Code

There's a common misconception among low- to middle-class households that wealthy people get rich by exploiting the underprivileged.

Naturally, this isn't always the case, but in certain families, having little money puts you on par with the rest of your family or your neighbors.

There Is Only One "Good Life" That Needs Sacrifice

Are you aware of the sacrifices your parents made for you to play a musical instrument, attend a private school, or participate in your favorite sport?

This myth erroneously links hardship and sacrifice to wealth and prosperity. It is wholly incorrect.

Illness and Sadness Come with Wealth

A youngster may frequently see heated debates around money—or the lack of it.

Those hurtful recollections make money associated with undesirable feelings.

When you were a youngster, what lessons about money did your parents, teachers, and other adults teach you? Which of those signals is undermining your ability to make money?

Chapter 3

How to Develop a Financially Positive Attitude?

Have you ever considered the statement, "Making money is hard, and managing it is even harder?" Prosperity and wealth are unfit for individuals like me. Life is challenging.

Well, it is just untrue!

It's merely a self-perpetuated narrative that lives only in your mind.

Developing a more optimistic outlook on money is the first step towards accumulating more wealth in your life. Next, concentrate on strategies to increase your income and make prudent financial decisions.

As an illustration:

You'll discover that you're drawing it to you rather than avoiding it.

You will find it intriguing and enjoy the time you spend learning how to manage it more skillfully, as opposed to finding it tedious or challenging.

Your money balance will be exciting to check rather than something to be feared since it continues increasing!

That is the effect of having an optimistic outlook on money.

You may reap the rewards of cultivating a good money mentality for the rest of your life.

Chapter 4

How To Change Your Perception Of Money And Attract Wealth

I wanted to share with you three easy actions that you can follow now to break free from your money-limiting beliefs and realize your full potential for financial success.

List any limiting beliefs you might hold

These might be any of the many illusions about attracting wealth that we previously discussed, such as the idea that you need to make a lot of sacrifices to achieve financial independence or that money is a necessary condition for success.

Consider everything that has prevented you from reaching your goals and hindered your capacity to draw in wealth. After that, put that idea in writing and give it careful thought.

Use Verifiable Statements to Counter Your Limiting Beliefs

If you think it costs money to create money, for instance, keep in mind that you can start a lot of enterprises, including consulting, network marketing, or becoming a service provider, for less than $550.

As an alternative, you could be eligible for a raise and promotion if you enroll in your company's complimentary management training program.

Draft an Upbeat Reversal Statement

"Everything I need to make money is showing up easily at no cost to me" is a possible sentence to write.

Declare this aloud many times a day for a minimum of thirty days, and this conviction will inexorably become ingrained in your financial outlook.

It's crucial to see yourself with money if you want to attract it.

Clearly define your financial objectives

One of the most important steps in developing a healthy money mentality is setting financial objectives.

When establishing your financial objectives, make every effort to be as explicit as you can. You may want to use the SMART goal-setting template, which stands for specific, Measurable, Achievable, Relevant, and Time-bound.

Setting these objectives can help you view money differently and provide you with a particular aim to strive toward.

Put Your Daily Affirmations Into Practice

To teach ourselves to think and speak positively about money requires time and persistent work.

You may help attract the chances, resources, and people who can assist you in achieving your financial objectives by utilizing daily affirmations.

Ask for what you want consistently, and then give the universe the reins to figure out how to give it to you.

Chapter 5

Affirmations To Attract Money And Grow Your Wealth

Let's now have a look at some affirmations you may use regularly to help you overcome your money-related limiting beliefs and become more receptive to the boundless riches the universe desires for you.

I want you to repeat these affirmations for 30 days straight, at least once a day (two is ideal), so you might want to jot them down as you go.

Give them a month to become a regular part of your routine.

I am Making Wise Decisions Regarding My Financial Assets

Try to picture yourself in that situation.

You're keeping an eye on your spending and making prudent financial decisions rather than squandering cash on things you don't need.

As a consequence, your bills are being paid off, your money account is increasing, and all of a sudden, your lofty goals—like taking that dream trip, paying off your home, or retiring early—seem more realistic.

After reading this chapter, take a minute to reflect on the financial decisions you now make.

Consider the following questions for yourself:

- How can you earn more while spending less?
- Is it time to ask for a promotion or increase your rates?
- What about your patterns of spending?
- What are some strategies you may use to cut down on the amount of money you spend needlessly every month?

Imagine yourself making a deliberate effort to save, invest, and handle your finances more skillfully.

I am earning all the money I require to fulfill all of my life's ambitions

Imagine having more than enough income to live comfortably and never having to worry about missing a bill payment.

No more debt, no more wondering about how you're going to pay for that big, unforeseen purchase, and no more stress about making ends meet.

You are far closer to that truth than you realize, and that is what I want you to know right now.

Imagine yourself in that situation right now, receiving a bill in the mail and being so appreciative that you can pay for it at that same moment.

Alternatively, accept an invitation to go on a fantastic vacation without hesitation as you are certain you can afford it.

Experience the thankfulness, self-assurance, and liberation that follows!

A great deal of the bad energy you have surrounding money will go if you repeat this affirmation daily.

I am letting go of all negative money-related thoughts and am at ease to see my dreams come true

It's time to let go of your constrictive financial ideas.

They are preventing you from developing into the person you were intended to be. Experience your strength and limitless potential.

You are capable of achieving all your life's goals. The money you need to turn your vision into a reality WILL come to you as you strive toward your goals. I promise it.

The current status of your bank account is nothing more than the physical manifestation of your previous thinking," asserts Bob Proctor.

I wholeheartedly concur with it. Your bank account balance will drastically change if you alter the way you think about money. Promised.

Activate Your Affirmations to Draw Wealth

You may raise your consciousness and cultivate a positive money attitude by using affirmations, making decisions about what you want, acting as though it's feasible, and believing it.

The truth is that with deliberate effort, you can attract riches into your life.

You will draw all wealth to yourself through the Law of Attraction.

CHAPTER 6

Introduction to the Poverty Mindset: Awakening the Mind

In the journey toward financial transformation, one of the first and most significant hurdles to overcome is the poverty mindset. This deeply ingrained set of beliefs and thought patterns can act as a formidable barrier, often limiting individuals from realizing their full potential and breaking free from the cycle of poverty. In this chapter, we delve into the intricacies of the poverty mindset, exploring its origins, manifestations, and the pivotal role of awareness in awakening the mind to new possibilities.

Defining the Poverty Mindset

At its core, the poverty mindset is a collection of attitudes and beliefs that shape an individual's perception of wealth, success, and personal worth. It goes beyond mere financial limitations, encompassing a psychological and emotional framework that can perpetuate a sense of lack and scarcity even in the absence of tangible constraints. The poverty mindset can manifest in various ways, such as a fear of taking risks, a reluctance to invest in personal development, and a tendency to view success as elusive or unattainable.

Unraveling the Roots of Limiting Beliefs

To effectively address the poverty mindset, it is crucial to unravel the roots of limiting beliefs that have taken hold over time. These beliefs often stem from early childhood experiences, societal conditioning, or a series of setbacks that create a narrative of scarcity. Whether inherited from family circumstances or developed through exposure to economic hardships, these limiting beliefs can become deeply embedded in the subconscious, influencing decision-making and shaping one's perception of what is achievable.

The Power of Mindfulness and Gratitude

Awakening the mind begins with mindfulness—a deliberate awareness of one's thoughts, emotions, and the impact of these on behavior. In this section, we explore the transformative power of mindfulness in breaking free from the chains of the poverty mindset. Through practices such as meditation and self-reflection, individuals can develop an acute awareness of their thought patterns, enabling them to challenge and reframe limiting beliefs.

Gratitude, as a complementary practice, plays a pivotal role in shifting focus from scarcity to abundance. By consciously acknowledging and appreciating the positive aspects of life, individuals can gradually cultivate a mindset that sees opportunities rather than obstacles, fostering a sense of empowerment and resilience.

Cultivating a Positive and Open Mindset

Cultivating a positive and open mindset is a continuous process of self-discovery and intentional growth. This involves replacing negative self-talk with affirming language, embracing a "can-do" attitude, and consciously choosing optimism over pessimism. The chapter concludes with insights into practical strategies for fostering a positive mindset, setting the stage for the subsequent chapters that will delve into the concrete actions necessary to break free from the shackles of the poverty mindset.

In the quest for financial well-being, the journey begins with a single step—a step toward awakening the mind to new possibilities, challenging deeply ingrained beliefs, and laying the foundation for a mindset that paves the way for prosperity and abundance.

CHAPTER 7

The Power of Mindfulness and Awakening the Mind

In the pursuit of personal and financial transformation, the exploration of the mind takes center stage. One of the most transformative tools in this introspective journey is the tandem of mindfulness and gratitude. This chapter delves into the profound impact these practices can have in awakening the mind from the slumber of a poverty mindset, ushering in a new era of self-awareness, resilience, and abundance.

Understanding Mindfulness: A Gateway to Self-Awareness

Mindfulness, rooted in ancient contemplative traditions, has emerged as a powerful practice in the modern world. At its essence, mindfulness involves the cultivation of heightened awareness, paying deliberate attention to the present moment without judgment. In the context of awakening the mind from a poverty mindset, mindfulness serves as a gateway to self-awareness.

Through mindfulness practices such as meditation and mindful breathing, individuals can observe their thoughts and emotions without becoming entangled in them. This detachment allows for a clearer understanding of the patterns of thinking that contribute to a sense of scarcity. As individuals become more attuned to their mental landscape, they gain the capacity to challenge and reshape limiting beliefs, paving the way for a more empowered mindset.

Gratitude as a Transformative Force

Parallel to mindfulness, gratitude emerges as a transformative force capable of shifting focus from what is lacking to what is present. Gratitude is not merely a polite acknowledgment of positive aspects; it is a profound recognition and appreciation for the abundance that exists in one's life, irrespective of external circumstances.

The practice of gratitude involves consciously acknowledging and expressing appreciation for the small and significant blessings be it relationships, opportunities, or personal strengths. By actively engaging in gratitude exercises, individuals begin to rewire their neural pathways, fostering a positive outlook and an openness to abundance. Gratitude serves as a counterbalance to the scarcity mindset, redirecting attention toward the potential for growth and fulfillment.

Integration of Mindfulness and Gratitude

The synergy between mindfulness and gratitude becomes particularly potent when integrated into daily life. Mindfulness provides the awareness needed to catch and redirect negative thought patterns, while gratitude infuses each moment with a sense of appreciation and possibility.

Daily mindfulness practices, whether brief meditation sessions or mindful pauses during daily activities, become anchors for self-reflection and course correction. Pairing these practices with a gratitude journal, where one regularly records moments of appreciation, creates a positive feedback loop, reinforcing the mindset shift from scarcity to abundance.

The Ripple Effect on Decision-Making and Well-being

The impact of mindfulness and gratitude extends beyond mere mindset shifts; it influences decision-making and overall well-being. As individuals become more present and appreciative, they are better equipped to make decisions aligned with their goals and values. The reduction of stress and anxiety associated with a poverty mindset contributes to improved mental and emotional health.

Moreover, the ripple effect of a mindful and grateful approach touches not only the individual but also their interactions with others. Positive relationships and a sense of connectedness often emerge, creating a supportive environment conducive to personal and financial growth.

In conclusion, the power of mindfulness and gratitude lies in their ability to awaken the mind from the grip of a poverty mindset. These practices provide the tools necessary for individuals to navigate their thoughts, emotions, and perceptions, fostering a profound shift toward abundance and empowerment. As the journey unfolds, the integration of mindfulness and gratitude becomes a cornerstone, propelling individuals toward a future characterized by conscious decision-making, resilience, and a deep appreciation for the richness of life.

Self-Reflection: Identifying Limiting Beliefs

In the intricate tapestry of personal development and financial transformation, the process of self-reflection emerges as a crucial thread. At the heart of this introspective journey lies the profound task of identifying and unraveling limiting beliefs—the deeply ingrained thought patterns that act as invisible shackles, constraining one's potential and perpetuating the stronghold of a poverty mindset. In this chapter, we explore the transformative power of self-reflection, dissecting the layers of consciousness to expose and dismantle the limiting beliefs that stifle growth and prosperity.

The Mirror of Self-Reflection: A Catalyst for Change

Self-reflection serves as a metaphorical mirror, allowing individuals to gaze into the recesses of their minds and examine the beliefs that shape their perceptions of themselves and the world. This process requires a willingness to be introspective, to question the origins of one's beliefs, and to confront the uncomfortable truths that may have been buried in the subconscious.

Through self-reflection, individuals embark on a journey of self-discovery, peeling back the layers of conditioning and societal influences to reveal the core beliefs that dictate their actions and decisions. The mirror of self-reflection becomes a catalyst for change, enabling individuals to consciously choose which beliefs to reinforce and which to release.

Unmasking the Origins of Limiting Beliefs

Limiting beliefs often have roots that extend deep into the past, originating from childhood experiences, societal expectations, or repeated failures. Unmasking these origins is a pivotal step in understanding the narrative that has shaped one's mindset. It involves revisiting pivotal moments, acknowledging the impact of influential figures, and recognizing the stories that have been internalized over time.

The process of unmasking limiting beliefs requires a delicate balance of compassion and honesty. It involves acknowledging the circumstances that may have contributed to the formation of these beliefs while recognizing that they do not define one's worth or potential. Self-reflection becomes a tool for rewriting the narrative, allowing individuals to take authorship of their stories and create a new, empowering script for their lives.

Challenging the Validity of Limiting Beliefs

Once identified, limiting beliefs must be subjected to scrutiny. Are these beliefs based on objective truths, or are they distorted perceptions shaped by past experiences? This phase of self-reflection involves challenging the validity of limiting beliefs, dissecting them to discern between fact and fiction.

Engaging in a dialogue with oneself, individuals can question the evidence supporting these beliefs and explore alternative perspectives. This process requires a curious and open mindset, inviting a willingness to entertain new possibilities and reinterpret past experiences. As the layers of distortion are peeled away, individuals gain clarity on the falsehoods that have held them captive, opening the door to a more liberated and expansive mindset.

The Liberating Power of Reconstructing Beliefs

The ultimate goal of self-reflection is not only to identify and challenge limiting beliefs but to actively reconstruct them into empowering narratives. This involves consciously choosing new beliefs that align with aspirations, values, and the vision for a more abundant future.

Reconstructing beliefs is a dynamic process that requires consistent effort and reinforcement. Affirmations, visualization, and intentional language play crucial roles in this transformation. By adopting a proactive stance in reshaping their internal dialogue, individuals cultivate a mindset that supports their goals and aspirations, gradually replacing scarcity with a sense of abundance.

In conclusion, the journey of self-reflection in identifying and dismantling limiting beliefs is a pivotal aspect of awakening the mind from the clutches of a poverty mindset. It is a courageous exploration into the depths of one's consciousness, a process that demands honesty, compassion, and a commitment to personal growth. As the layers of limiting beliefs are shed, individuals emerge with a renewed sense of self, poised to embrace a mindset that paves the way for financial prosperity and a more fulfilling life.

Cultivating a Positive and Open Mindset: Awakening the Mind

In the intricate dance of personal development, the cultivation of a positive and open mindset stands as a beacon of transformative power. As individuals navigate the terrain of their thoughts and emotions, this chapter explores the profound impact of fostering positivity and openness, shedding light on how these qualities serve as catalysts for breaking free from the clutches of a poverty mindset and ushering in a new era of abundance.

The Seeds of Positivity: Nurturing Growth Amid Challenges

At the core of cultivating a positive mindset lies the acknowledgment that challenges are inherent in the human experience. It's not about eliminating adversity but rather about developing the resilience and optimism to navigate challenges with grace. By viewing obstacles as opportunities for growth, individuals begin to plant the seeds of positivity in the fertile soil of their minds.

This cultivation involves a conscious choice to focus on solutions rather than problems, to see setbacks as stepping stones rather than roadblocks. Embracing a positive mindset doesn't negate the existence of difficulties; rather, it empowers individuals to approach challenges with a mindset that seeks learning, adaptation, and growth.

The Role of Language: Shaping Thoughts and Reality

Language serves as a powerful tool in shaping thoughts and, consequently, one's reality.

Cultivating a positive mindset involves a deliberate shift in the language one uses both internally and externally. By replacing self-limiting and negative language with affirming and empowering statements, individuals contribute to the creation of a mental landscape that fosters optimism and possibility.

Positive affirmations, when consistently integrated into daily life, act as a steady stream of encouragement, challenging and reshaping ingrained thought patterns. Language becomes a vessel for manifesting positive beliefs, reinforcing the idea that abundance is not just an external condition but a state of mind.

Embracing an Open Mindset: Welcoming Possibilities

An open mindset is characterized by a receptivity to new ideas, a willingness to adapt, and an eagerness to embrace change. In the context of financial transformation, an open mindset is a key component of breaking free from the limitations imposed by a poverty mindset. It involves challenging preconceived notions about what is possible and opening oneself to a world of opportunities.

Embracing an open mindset requires a departure from a fixed view of oneself and the world. It invites individuals to question assumptions, explore alternative perspectives, and remain curious in the face of uncertainty. This openness becomes a gateway to innovation, creativity, and the discovery of pathways to prosperity that may have previously gone unnoticed.

Resilience in the Face of Adversity: The Heartbeat of Positivity

Cultivating a positive mindset is not a shield against adversity; rather, it is the heartbeat that sustains resilience in the face of challenges. The ability to bounce back from setbacks, view failures as learning experiences, and maintain optimism amid difficulties is a testament to the strength of a positive mindset.

Resilience is nurtured through a combination of mindset, coping strategies, and a support system. The cultivation of a positive mindset acts as a cornerstone in building this resilience, enabling individuals to navigate financial uncertainties with a sense of inner strength and a belief that they possess the capacity to overcome obstacles.

Integration into Daily Life: A Mindset Shift

The true power of cultivating a positive and open mindset lies in its integration into daily life. It is not a temporary state but a continuous, intentional practice that permeates thoughts, actions, and interactions. This integration involves mindfulness in language, a commitment to learning and growth, and a conscious effort to approach challenges with an optimistic lens.

As individuals cultivate a positive and open mindset, they contribute not only to their personal well-being but also to the creation of a more resilient and vibrant community. Positivity becomes contagious, and the collective shift in mindset becomes a catalyst for broader societal change.

In conclusion, the journey of awakening the mind through the cultivation of a positive and open mindset is a profound exploration into the realms of thoughts and beliefs. It is a dynamic process that involves nurturing positivity amid challenges, shaping language to reinforce empowering beliefs, embracing an open mindset, and fostering resilience in the face of adversity. As individuals embark on this transformative journey, they sow the seeds of a mindset that not only liberates them from the constraints of a poverty mindset but also paves the way for a life rich in possibilities and abundance.

Chapter 8

Understanding Your Money Story

Unpacking Your Financial Backpack

Let's start with a simple truth: the way we perceive and interact with money today is deeply rooted in our past. Your upbringing, early experiences, and the stories you absorbed as a kid create the foundation of your current financial mindset. This chapter is all about unzipping that mental backpack you've been carrying and taking a closer look at the treasures and baggage you've accumulated.

Influence of Upbringing: The Family Finance Classroom

Remember those childhood days when you played "store" with monopoly money or tagged along with your parents to the grocery store? Little did you know, you were enrolled in the unofficial Family Finance 101 class. Your family, whether intentionally or not, became your first financial influencers.

In this section, we'll delve into the influence of your upbringing on your money mindset. Were your parents frugal savers or carefree spenders? Did money conversations revolve around abundance or scarcity? These early impressions often become the building blocks of our financial beliefs.

Family Money Portrait Take a moment to sketch a portrait of your family's approach to money when you were growing up. Jot down memories of discussions about money, observed spending habits, and any impactful events related to finances. This exercise is your first step in understanding the roots of your money story.

The Money Whisperers: Past Influencers

As we grew, our circle of influence expanded beyond the family unit. Teachers, friends, and even media characters became the unintentional narrators of our financial script. The messages we received from these external sources often reinforced or challenged the beliefs we picked up at home.

External Influencers Diary Create a diary of external influencers. Who were the people or characters that shaped your views on money outside of your family? Recall conversations, movies, or books that left a lasting impression. This exercise will help you identify additional layers of influence that have shaped your money story.

Identifying Your Money Beliefs: The Hidden Scripts

Now that we've opened the treasure chest of your past, let's shine a light on the scripts those silent narratives that play in the background of your mind, influencing your financial decisions without you even realizing it.

Your Money Beliefs Inventory List down your current beliefs about money. Are they empowering or limiting? For example, do you believe that money is hard to come by, or do you believe in the abundance of financial opportunities? This exercise is like holding a mirror to your subconscious, revealing the beliefs that might be holding you back.

Analyzing Your Money Story: From Observation to Action

Understanding your money story is not about placing blame or dwelling on the past. It's about awareness and empowerment. Now that you've uncovered the threads of your financial narrative, let's weave them into a tapestry of understanding.

Evaluate the impact of your money story on your current financial situation. How have these early influences shaped your spending habits, your approach to saving, and your relationship with money in general? This exercise is a bridge between awareness and action, allowing you to see the direct links between your past and present financial behaviors.

Moving Forward: Your Money Story Makeover

Congratulations! You've just taken the first step on the path to transforming your relationship with money. By understanding your money story, you're laying the foundation for a Money Magnet Mindset. In the next chapters, we'll delve into the art of shifting limiting beliefs, setting clear financial goals, and unleashing the power of positive affirmations.

As you close this chapter, take a moment to reflect on the insights gained. Your money story is a powerful tool, not a limitation. It's the clay from which you can mold a new financial reality. Remember, you're not rewriting history; you're creating a future where your money story is one of empowerment, abundance, and conscious wealth creation.

So, here's to you, the archaeologist of your own financial past! Keep that curiosity alive as we venture into the heart of the Money Magnet Mindset journey. The best is yet to come!

Chapter 9

Mindset Magic—Paving the Way to Financial Prosperity

In the pursuit of financial success, one often stumbles on a fundamental truth: it all begins within the mind. This notion might appear simple on the surface, yet its implications are profound and transformative. The foundation for this grand endeavor is your mindset, the lens through which you perceive, interpret and interact with the financial world.

Imagine for a moment that your mind is the powerful engine of a finely crafted car. You're filled with potential, and you know that you're capable of propelling yourself toward financial success at breakneck speed. Just as a skilled driver can navigate challenging terrain and accelerate toward their destination, your mindset has the power to steer you through the twists and turns of the financial world, turning obstacles into opportunities.

But what exactly do I mean when I say that your mindset is the foundational building block of your success? And if it's so important, then why doesn't everyone possess this mindset to make themselves successful?

Navigating Mindset: Your Path to Success

At its core, mindset is the collection of beliefs, attitudes, and perceptions that govern how you approach life's challenges and opportunities. It's the engine under the hood, determining your financial decisions, fueling your financial habits, and ultimately defining your financial destiny. In the context of finances, your mindset can either be the turbocharged force that propels you forward or the sluggish anchor that holds you back.

Consider two individuals with similar financial circumstances: one embraces a mindset of abundance, viewing financial challenges as stepping stones to growth, while the other is ensnared by a scarcity mindset. They see every obstacle as an insurmountable barrier and an excuse for failure. The difference in their financial trajectories is expected to differ greatly. And it's all because of our differing mindsets.

The concept of mindset transcends mere psychology; it holds profound implications for your financial future. Your mindset determines your financial decisions, shapes your financial habits, and ultimately defines your financial destiny. It can propel you toward abundance and success or keep you mired in financial struggle and frustration.

Research has shown that individuals with a growth-oriented mindset, one that thrives on learning, adaptability, and resilience, are more likely to be successful (Baer, 2014). On the contrary, those entrenched in a fixed mindset, where they perceive their abilities and circumstances as static, tend to limit their financial potential.

In this chapter, we're going to talk about all the things that are keeping you from developing the kind of mindset that will allow you to achieve everything you want. We will uncover the dream killers lurking within your character—the ones that limit your potential and inhibit your growth. These dream killers, often masquerading as limiting beliefs, have the potential to sabotage your aspirations, stifle your potential, and hinder your path to financial success.

Prepare to challenge your preconceptions, question your long-held beliefs, and embark on a journey of self-discovery and transformation. As we unravel the mysteries of the mind and its profound impact on your financial destiny, you'll gain the insights and tools necessary to break free from the constraints of limiting beliefs and chart a course toward the financial success you deserve. The time has come to harness the immense power of your mindset, to silence the dream killers, and to unleash your full potential on the path to financial prosperity.

Chapter 10

Online Business and Money-Making

Choosing the Right Online Business for Parents In today's digital age, more and more parents are looking for ways to earn an income while still being able to prioritize their family's needs. With the rise of online businesses, the opportunities for parents to achieve nancial freedom and exibility have never been greater. However, with so many options available, it can be overwhelming to know where to start. That's why it's crucial to choose the right online business that aligns with your skills, interests, and lifestyle.

One popular online business venture for parents is freelancing. Whether you have a background in writing, graphic design, web development, or marketing, freelancing allows you to work on your own terms and schedule. With numerous freelance platforms available, nding clients and building a portfolio has become easier than ever before.

Passive Income for Parents: Side Hustles That Work While You Parent

Passive Income for Parents: Side Hustles That Work While You Parent Another lucrative option is starting your own e-commerce business or dropshipping. This involves creating an online store and selling products without the need for inventory.

With dropshipping, you can focus on marketing and customer service while suppliers handle shipping and inventory management. This business model allows parents to have a hands-on role in their venture while still having the exibility to work from home.

For those parents who are more interested in generating passive income, af liate marketing can be an excellent choice. By promoting products or services on your website or social media platforms, you earn a commission for every sale made through your unique af liate link. This business model requires upfront effort in creating content and building an audience but can eventually lead to a steady stream of passive income.

Additionally, if you have a skill or expertise that can be taught, creating and selling online courses can be a pro table venture. Parents often have a wealth of knowledge and experience that others are willing to pay to learn. Platforms like Udemy and Teachable make it easy to create and sell courses, allowing you to reach a global audience.

When choosing the right online business, it's important to consider your nancial goals, time availability, and personal interests. Research different niches and business models to nd the one that suits you best. Remember, success in any online business requires dedication, perseverance, and continuous learning. With the right mindset and determination, you can create a thriving online business that works while you parent.

Passive Income for Parents: Side Hustles That Work While You Parent

Passive Income for Parents: Side Hustles That Work While You Parent Whether you are a single mother, unemployed, or simply looking to supplement your income, the world of online business offers endless opportunities. By choosing the right online business for parents, you can achieve nancial independence while still being able to prioritize your family's needs. Don't be afraid to take the leap and start your online business journey today.

Creating a Website or Blog to Generate Passive Income In today's digital age, creating a website or blog has become a popular and effective way to generate passive income. Whether you are a parent, a single mother, or currently unemployed, starting your own online business can provide you with the exibility and nancial stability you need. This subchapter will guide you through the process of setting up a website or blog that can become a reliable source of passive income.

Firstly, it is crucial to determine your target audience and niche. Understand your interests, skills, and expertise, and identify a specic audience that you can cater to. This will help you develop content that resonates with your readers and attracts potential customers or clients.

Next, choose a hosting platform and domain name for your website. There are numerous options available, such as WordPress, Wix, or Squarespace, each offering various features and customization options. Select a domain name that is memorable, relevant to your niche, and easy to spell. This will help in building a strong online presence.

Once your website is set up, focus on creating high-quality and engaging content.

Regularly update your blog with articles, tutorials, product reviews, or any other content that aligns with your niche. Remember to optimize your content for search engines by incorporating relevant keywords and backlinks to improve your website's visibility.

Passive Income for Parents: Side Hustles That Work While You Parent

Passive Income for Parents: Side Hustles That Work While You Parent To monetize your website, consider various income streams. One popular option is af liate marketing, where you promote products or services and earn a commission for every sale made through your unique af liate link. Another option is to display advertisements on your website, either through Google AdSense or directly partnering with brands. Additionally, you can offer digital products, such as e-books, online courses, or exclusive content, that users can purchase.

Lastly, focus on driving traf c to your website. Utilize social media platforms, email marketing, and search engine optimization techniques to increase your website's visibility. Engage with your audience through comments, social media interactions, and newsletters to build a loyal following.

Creating a website or blog to generate passive income requires dedication and consistent effort, but the rewards can be substantial. By providing valuable content, optimizing your website for monetization, and driving traf c, you can successfully create a lucrative online business that ts seamlessly into your parenting responsibilities or personal circumstances.

Monetizing Your Online Content through Af liate Marketing In today's digital age, the internet offers endless opportunities to earn money from the comfort of your own home. One lucrative avenue for parents, single mothers, and the unemployed is af liate marketing. This subchapter will guide you through the world of af liate marketing, explaining how you can leverage your online content to generate passive income.

Passive Income for Parents: Side Hustles That Work While You Parent

Passive Income for Parents: Side Hustles That Work While You Parent Af liate marketing involves promoting products or services on your website, blog, or social media platforms. When someone purchases a product through your unique affiliate link, you earn a commission. This method is ideal for parents and single mothers who want a flexible way to earn money while caring for their children or managing household responsibilities.

To get started with affiliate marketing, you need to find a niche that aligns with your interests and expertise. Online business and money-making guides, entrepreneurship and start-up guides, freelancing and remote work guides, e-commerce and dropshipping guides, and passive income and side hustle guides are all popular niches that cater to your target audience. Choose a niche that resonates with you and allows you to create valuable content that your audience will find useful.

Once you've chosen your niche, it's time to sign up for affiliate programs. Many companies offer affiliate programs, including Amazon, ClickBank, and ShareASale.

Research and select programs that offer products or services related to your niche. It's crucial to choose reputable programs that provide fair commissions and have a solid track record.

Next, create high-quality content that incorporates your affiliate links naturally. Whether it's blog posts, social media posts, or videos, focus on providing valuable information to your audience while subtly promoting the products or services you are affiliated with.

Transparency is key – always disclose your af liate relationships to maintain trust with your audience.

Passive Income for Parents: Side Hustles That Work While You Parent

Passive Income for Parents: Side Hustles That Work While You Parent To maximize your earnings, consider diversifying your afliate marketing efforts. Promote a range of products or services within your niche, and experiment with different marketing strategies to see what works best for you. Keep track of your results and adjust your approach as needed.

Remember, afliate marketing is not a get-rich-quick scheme. It takes time, dedication, and consistent effort to build a successful afliate marketing business. However, with perseverance, you can create a reliable source of passive income that allows you to provide for your family while enjoying the exibility and freedom of working from home.

In conclusion, af liate marketing offers an excellent opportunity for parents, single mothers, and the unemployed to monetize their online content. By choosing a niche, signing up for reputable af liate programs, creating valuable content, and diversifying your efforts, you can start generating passive income and building a successful online business.

Selling Digital Products or Services Online

In today's digital age, the opportunities to generate income online are endless. As a parent, single mother, or someone who is currently unemployed, harnessing the power of the internet can provide you with a viable source of income while still allowing you to focus on your parenting responsibilities. In this subchapter, we will explore the world of selling digital products or services online and how it can be the perfect side hustle for you.

Passive Income for Parents: Side Hustles That Work While You Parent

Passive Income for Parents: Side Hustles That Work While You Parent With the rise of online business and money-making guides, entrepreneurship and startup guides, freelancing and remote work guides, e-commerce and dropshipping guides, as well as passive income and side hustle guides, it's clear that the demand for knowledge in this eld is on the rise. This is a testament to the countless success stories of individuals who have taken advantage of the digital economy to create nancial stability and freedom for themselves.

One of the most attractive aspects of selling digital products or services online is the low startup costs and the ability to work from anywhere. Whether you have a knack for graphic design, writing, photography, or even teaching, there is a market for your skills online. You can create digital products such as e-books, online courses, stock photos, or even software applications. Alternatively, you can offer services like freelance writing, virtual assistance, social media management, or consulting.

To get started, it's crucial to identify your target audience and understand their needs and pain points. Conduct thorough market research to determine what digital products or services are in demand. Once you have a clear understanding of your niche, you can start creating your product or service.

Building a strong online presence is essential for attracting potential customers. Utilize social media platforms, create a professional website, and engage with your audience through informative content and valuable insights.

Passive Income for Parents: Side Hustles That Work While You Parent

Passive Income for Parents: Side Hustles That Work While You Parent Nowadays, there are numerous platforms available that can help you sell your digital products or services. Some of the popular options include Etsy, Shopify, Gumroad, or even creating your own website with integrated e-commerce capabilities. Choose the platform that aligns with your goals and budget.

In conclusion, selling digital products or services online can be a lucrative side hustle for parents, single mothers, and the unemployed. With the right knowledge, skills, and dedication, you can harness the power of the internet to create a sustainable source of income while still focusing on your parenting responsibilities. So, why wait?

Start exploring the world of online entrepreneurship today and unlock your nancial potential.

Building an Email List and Utilizing Email Marketing Strategies

In today's digital age, email marketing has become an essential tool for businesses and entrepreneurs alike. It allows you to connect with your audience on a personal level, build trust, and ultimately grow your online business. This subchapter will guide you through the process of building an email list and utilizing effective email marketing strategies to generate passive income while you parent.

For parents, single mothers, and the unemployed, email marketing offers a exible and low-cost way to start a side hustle or launch an online business. Whether you're interested in freelancing, e-commerce, or creating passive income streams, having a solid email list will be the foundation of your success.

Passive Income for Parents: Side Hustles That Work While You Parent

Passive Income for Parents: Side Hustles That Work While You Parent Firstly, we'll explore the importance of building an email list. Your email list is a valuable asset that allows you to reach your target audience directly. By offering a lead magnet, such as a free e-book, checklist, or webinar, you can entice your audience to sign up for your newsletter. We'll discuss various lead magnet ideas and how to create compelling opt-in forms to maximize conversions.

Next, we'll delve into the strategies for growing your email list. We'll cover organic methods like content marketing, guest blogging, and social media promotion, as well as paid methods such as Facebook advertising and in uencer partnerships. You'll learn how to optimize your website for lead generation and leverage the power of landing pages and pop-ups to capture email addresses effectively.

Once you have a growing email list, we'll move on to email marketing strategies. You'll discover how to craft engaging and personalized emails that resonate with your audience, nurture relationships, and drive conversions. We'll explore different types of email campaigns, including welcome sequences, promotional offers, and automated follow-ups, to maximize your email marketing efforts.

Additionally, we'll discuss the importance of segmentation and targeting in email marketing. By dividing your email list into different segments based on demographics, interests, or behavior, you can deliver highly relevant content and offers to each group.

We'll also explore the power of automation and how it can save you time and increase your revenue.

Passive Income for Parents: Side Hustles That Work While You Parent

Passive Income for Parents: Side Hustles That Work While You Parent By the end of this subchapter, you'll have a deep understanding of building an email list and utilizing effective email marketing strategies. You'll be equipped with the knowledge and tools to generate passive income while you parent, whether through freelancing, e-commerce, or other online business ventures. Get ready to unlock the potential of email marketing and take your side hustle to new heights.

Tips for Scaling and Growing Your Online Business In today's digital age, more and more parents, single mothers, and the unemployed are turning to online businesses as a means of earning a reliable income. Whether you're looking to start a side hustle, dive into entrepreneurship, or make passive income, scaling and growing your online business is essential for long-term success. In this subchapter, we will explore some valuable tips that can help you achieve your goals and take your online business to the next level.

1. Define Your Vision: Before scaling your online business, it's crucial to have a clear vision of what you want to achieve. Set specific goals and outline a roadmap to track your progress. This will help you stay focused and motivated throughout your journey.

2. Build a Solid Foundation: A strong foundation is essential for scaling your online business. Invest time in creating a professional website, optimizing your online presence, and building a

solid brand identity. This will establish credibility and attract potential customers.

3. Leverage Social Media: Social media platforms are powerful tools for reaching a vast audience and growing your online business. Identify the platforms that resonate most with your target audience and develop a consistent presence. Engage with your followers, provide valuable content, and build a community around your brand.

Passive Income for Parents: Side Hustles That Work While You Parent

Passive Income for Parents: Side Hustles That Work While You Parent 4. Automate and Delegate: As a parent or a single mother, time is a precious resource.

Look for opportunities to automate repetitive tasks, such as email marketing or inventory management, to free up your time for more strategic activities. Additionally, consider delegating certain tasks to capable freelancers or virtual assistants.

5. Expand Your Product or Service Offerings: To scale your online business, consider diversifying your product or service offerings. Conduct market research to identify customer needs and develop new offerings that align with your brand. This will attract a wider customer base and increase your revenue streams.

6. Collaborate with Inuencers: Partnering with in uencers can signicantly boost your online business's visibility and credibility. Identify in uencers in your niche and reach out to them for

collaborations or sponsored content opportunities. Their endorsement can help you reach a wider audience and drive more sales.

7. Invest in Customer Experience: A satis ed customer is more likely to become a loyal one and recommend your business to others. Focus on providing exceptional customer service, personalized experiences, and prompt responses to inquiries or issues. Happy customers will not only generate repeat business but also spread positive word-of-mouth.

Scaling and growing your online business requires dedication, strategic planning, and continuous effort. By following these tips, you can pave the way towards building a successful online business that enables you to achieve nancial stability and exibility while ful lling your responsibilities as a parent or single mother.

Chapter 11

The Laws of Attraction

According to the law of attraction, ideas that are constructive lead to good things in life, while those that are destructive result in bad things. Its foundation is the idea that good energy attracts success in all spheres of life, including relationships, health, and economics, and that ideas are a type of energy.

What are the seven sub-laws of the Law of Attraction?

The law of attraction has seven sub-laws. Even if we don't believe any of these to be natural laws, there are some important insights. Check out what the seven laws of attraction have to offer here:

Phenomena:

The law of magnetism

It is explained by this sub-law that like attracts like. Positive and negative thoughts are attracted to each other in the same way. If we only maintain our pessimism, bad things will keep happening to us. However, if we look for the good things in life, we'll see things more clearly and find more uplifting experiences and possibilities, which will enhance our well-being.

Manifestation

To transform the present, this sub-law counsels us to concentrate our attention and efforts there. Change is not sparked by dwelling on the past or worrying about the future. But if we work hard now, we can build a better future and realize our aspirations.

The Appropriate Steps

We can alter or eliminate certain unpleasant aspects of our existence. Unhealthy relationships, toxic environments, or unfulfilling occupations can all impede our ability to lead meaningful lives.

We can fill the void left by eliminating these negatives with things that contribute to living more purposefully. Your life will be improved and enriched if you have a clear understanding of your mission and personal beliefs.

Mindful Balance

Though they can't all be, some days can be fantastic. Once in a while, you may stumble or face a setback. The fact is, that's just a fact of life. Recognizing our shortcomings is a good thing since it gives us a chance to grow. As we rejoice in our victories, we also need to acknowledge our losses.

Firm aspirations

Maintaining our attention on the objectives and aspirations that will enhance our lives is the main subject of this sub-law. Setting and achieving specific goals promotes greater health, professional success, and positive relationships.

We could go through a lot of changes as we go through different phases of life. To stay grounded, however, we must be aware of our feelings regarding our ideals and aspirations. Even though our beliefs and aspirations may change throughout our lives, maintaining a strong sense of self will support us in achieving our most significant objectives.

Resilience

Our energy can be influenced by the balance that's found in our surroundings. By focusing on the energy around us, we can stay optimistic and make progress toward our objectives. It is only to our advantage to surround ourselves with like-minded individuals who approach goal-achieving with the same mindset. They provide help, incentives, and encouragement.

Broad impact

The law of attraction is based on this. What we contribute to the world comes back to us. The way we treat other people has a direct effect on our lives. Disrespecting someone gives them more motivation to treat you poorly as well.

Additionally, if you're upbeat and diligent, others will want to live and work with you, which will improve community development and create a cozier, more enjoyable work environment. Recall that lending a helpful hand, even if you don't believe it would directly improve your life, can result in many great returns. By assisting others, think about bringing into the world what you wish to get from it.

Chapter 12

Receiving Money

Personal Payments: Receiving money from individuals for personal reasons, such as repayment of a debt, receiving a gift, or receiving payment for goods or services provided.

Salary and Wages: Receiving money as compensation for employment or services rendered. This includes regular paychecks, bonuses, commissions, or any other form of income earned through employment.

Business Transactions: Receiving money from customers or clients in exchange for products, services, or contracts. This can involve receiving payments through cash, checks, bank transfers, or electronic payment systems like credit cards or online payment platforms.

Investments and Returns: Receiving money from investments, such as dividends from stocks, interest payments from bonds or savings accounts, rental income from real estate properties, or capital gains from the sale of assets.

Government Benefits: Receiving money from government programs or benefits, such as pensions, social security payments, unemployment benefits, or welfare payments.

The specific method of receiving money may vary depending on the circumstances, the parties involved, and the available payment options. It can range from traditional methods like cash or checks to modern electronic payment systems, including bank transfers, online platforms, or mobile payment apps.

It is very important to note that before one can receive money, one must exchange a certain value for the money. This is known as the law of Exchange.

The law of exchange states that to receive money, one must provide something of value in return. This principle is fundamental to financial transactions and plays a significant role in the pursuit of financial freedom. Here's how the law of exchange connects to financial freedom and some additional laws and principles that support this assertion:

Value Creation: The law of exchange underscores the importance of creating value for others. To receive money, individuals must offer products, services, or solutions that address the needs and desires of others. By focusing on value creation, individuals can attract customers, clients, or employers who are willing to exchange money for the value they provide.

Entrepreneurship: The law of exchange is particularly relevant to entrepreneurship. Starting a business involves identifying a market need and developing products or services that fulfill that need. Successful entrepreneurs understand the importance of creating value and building mutually beneficial relationships with customers, which in turn leads to financial rewards and potential financial freedom.

Supply and Demand: The law of supply and demand is closely tied to the law of exchange. It states that the price of a product or service is determined by the balance between its availability (supply) and the desire for it (demand). Understanding supply and demand dynamics allows individuals to identify opportunities for offering products or services that are in high demand, enabling them to receive money in exchange for meeting that demand.

Law of Compensation: The law of compensation states that individuals are compensated in proportion to the value they provide. It emphasizes that financial rewards are often commensurate with the level of contribution, skill, and expertise offered. By continuously improving their skills and increasing their value to others, individuals can enhance their earning potential and move closer to financial freedom.

Law of Saving and Investing: The law of saving and investing highlights the importance of accumulating and growing wealth over time. It emphasizes the need to allocate a portion of earned money to savings and investments, allowing it to generate additional income and wealth through compounding. By adhering to this law, individuals can build a financial safety net and create opportunities for financial freedom in the future.

Law of Leverage: The law of leverage suggests that individuals can achieve more significant results by leveraging the resources, skills, and networks of others. Collaboration, partnerships, and delegation of tasks can amplify efforts and increase the potential for financial success. By using leverage strategically, individuals can accomplish more and accelerate their journey toward financial freedom.

Law of Continuous Learning: The law of continuous learning emphasizes the importance of ongoing personal and professional development. It suggests that individuals who invest in learning and acquiring new knowledge and skills have a higher likelihood of success and financial advancement. By staying adaptable, curious, and embracing lifelong learning, individuals can stay ahead of the curve, seize opportunities, and increase their earning potential.

8. Law of Persistence: The law of persistence reinforces the need for perseverance and

resilience in the pursuit of financial freedom. It recognizes that setbacks and obstacles are inevitable on the path to success. By maintaining a strong work ethic, staying focused on their goals, and persisting through challenges, individuals can overcome setbacks and ultimately achieve financial freedom.

By understanding and applying these laws and principles, individuals can navigate the world of finance more effectively, create value, and increase their chances of attaining financial freedom. They provide a framework for making wise financial decisions, building wealth, and ultimately creating a life of abundance and fulfillment.

Chapter 13

Expanding your Income Streams

Income streams refer to the various sources of income or revenue that individuals or businesses generate. Having multiple income streams can provide financial stability, diversify risk, and increase overall income. Here are some real-life examples of income streams: 1. Employment Income: This is the most common income stream, where individuals earn money through traditional employment. It includes salaries, wages, and bonuses received from working for an employer.

Self-Employment Income: Self-employment income is generated by individuals who run their businesses or work as freelancers, consultants, or contractors. They provide products or services directly to clients and customers and receive payment for their work.

Rental Income: Rental income is earned by owning and renting out properties such as apartments, houses, or commercial spaces. It can provide a consistent stream of cash flow from tenants' monthly rent payments.

Investment Income: Investment income is generated through various investment vehicles, such as stocks, bonds, mutual funds, or real estate. It includes dividends from stocks, interest from bonds or savings accounts, and capital gains from selling investments at a profit.

Royalties: Royalties are payments received by individuals or entities for the use of their intellectual property, such as copyrights, patents, or trademarks. Examples include royalties earned from books, music, artwork, or software.

Business Income: Business income is generated by owning and operating a business. It can come from sales of products or services, licensing agreements, franchise fees, or partnerships. Business owners have the potential to earn profits beyond their labor.

Affiliate Marketing: Affiliate marketing involves promoting and selling products or services on behalf of another company or individual. Affiliates earn a commission or a percentage of the sales generated through their referral links or promotional efforts.

8. Rental or Sharing Economy: With the rise of online platforms, individuals can generate income

by renting out their assets, such as vehicles, homes, or equipment. Examples include ride-sharing services, home-sharing platforms, and peer-to-peer lending.

Online Sales and E-commerce: Selling products or services online through platforms like e-commerce websites, online marketplaces, or creating digital products can generate income. This includes selling physical products, digital goods, e-books, courses, or offering services online.

Dividend Income: Dividend income is earned by owning stocks in companies that distribute a portion of their profits to shareholders. Dividends are typically paid regularly and can provide a steady income stream.

These are just a few examples of income streams, and individuals can combine multiple streams to diversify their income sources and increase their financial stability. It's important to note that the feasibility and profitability of each income stream may vary depending on factors such as location, market conditions, individual skills, and resources.

Expanding your income streams can be a smart strategy to enhance your financial stability, increase your earning potential, and create more opportunities for wealth accumulation. Here are some steps to consider when expanding your income streams:

Assess Your Skills and Interests: Begin by evaluating your skills, expertise, and interests. Identify areas where you have knowledge or experience that can be monetized. Consider both your professional skills and any hobbies or passions that can be turned into income-generating opportunities.

Research Income Opportunities: Conduct thorough research to explore different income opportunities that align with your skills and interests. Look for industries or niches that are growing, have demand, or offer potential for profitability. Consider both traditional and emerging sectors, as well as online platforms and marketplaces.

Diversify within Your Field: If you already have a primary income stream, consider ways to diversify within your existing field. Look for complementary services or products you can offer to your current customers or clients. For example, if you are a web designer, you could expand your services to include website maintenance or graphic design.

Leverage the Sharing Economy: The sharing economy has opened up numerous income opportunities. Consider ways to leverage platforms like Airbnb, Uber, TaskRabbit, or Upwork to generate additional income. These platforms allow you to monetize assets, skills, or spare time.

Develop Passive Income Streams: Passive income streams can provide ongoing revenue with minimal effort once set up. Explore options such as rental properties, dividend-paying investments, peer-to-peer lending, or creating digital products like e-books or online courses. These can generate income even when you're not actively working.

Start a Side Business: Launching a side business can be an effective way to diversify your income. Identify a market need or solve a problem with a product or service you can offer. Start small and gradually grow your business over time, leveraging your existing network or online platforms to reach a wider audience.

Explore Affiliate Marketing: Affiliate marketing allows you to earn a commission by promoting other people's products or services. Find affiliate programs that align with your interests or niche and promote them through your website, blog, social media channels, or email marketing.

Invest in Yourself: Continuously invest in your skills and knowledge to expand your income opportunities. Take courses, attend workshops or seminars, or acquire certifications that enhance your expertise and increase your market value. This can open doors to higher-paying jobs, consulting opportunities, or entrepreneurial ventures.

Network and Collaborate: Build relationships with like-minded individuals in your industry or related fields. Collaborate with others on joint ventures, partnerships, or projects that can create new income streams. Networking can also lead to referrals or new business opportunities.

Monitor and Adjust: Regularly assess the performance of your various income streams. Track the profitability, time commitment, and satisfaction derived from each stream. Be open to adjusting or eliminating income streams that are not yielding the desired results and focus on those that show growth potential.

Remember, expanding your income streams requires effort, persistence, and a willingness to take calculated risks. It's important to strike a balance between diversification and maintaining focus to ensure that your efforts are sustainable and aligned with your long-term goals.

Chapter 14

Leveraging Your Skills and Talents

To leverage one's skills and talents means to make the most effective use of them to achieve desired outcomes or goals. It involves recognizing and understanding one's unique abilities, strengths, and expertise and finding ways to apply them strategically and to their fullest potential. When you leverage your skills and talents, you are essentially using them as valuable resources to create opportunities, solve problems, and maximize your potential for success.

Leveraging your skills and talents is a powerful way to create income opportunities and maximize your earning potential. Here are some steps to effectively leverage your skills and talents:

Identify Your Skills and Talents: Take inventory of your skills, talents, and areas of expertise. Consider both hard skills (technical knowledge, specific abilities) and soft skills (communication, leadership, problem-solving). Reflect on what you enjoy doing and where you excel.

Understand Market Demand: Research the market demand for your skills and talents. Identify industries, sectors, or niches where your skills are in high demand. Look for opportunities where you can provide value and solve problems for individuals or businesses.

Define Your Unique Value Proposition: Determine what sets you apart from others who possess similar skills. Identify your unique strengths, experiences, or perspectives that differentiate you in the market. This will help you position yourself as a valuable asset to potential clients or employers.

Identify Target Audience or Market: Define your target audience or market based on your skills and talents. Determine who can benefit most from what you have to offer. Consider demographics, industries, or specific client segments that align with your expertise.

Develop a Personal Brand: Build a strong personal brand that showcases your skills, talents, and unique value proposition. Create a professional online presence through platforms like LinkedIn, a personal website, or a portfolio. Share your expertise through content creation, such as writing articles or creating videos, to establish yourself as an authority in your field.

Network and Collaborate: Network with individuals and businesses in your industry or related fields. Attend industry events, join professional associations, or participate in online communities. Collaborate on projects or partnerships that can help you expand your reach and tap into new opportunities.

Offer Freelance or Consulting Services: Consider offering your skills and talents as a freelancer or consultant. Freelancing allows you to work independently and offer your services on a project basis to clients. Consulting involves providing expert advice or solutions to businesses or individuals in need of your specific expertise.

Create and Monetize Your Products: Leverage your skills and talents to create and sell your products. This can include digital products like e-books, online courses, or software applications. You can also create physical products or merchandise based on your skills, such as artwork or handmade crafts.

Seek Career Advancement Opportunities: If you're currently employed, explore opportunities within your organization to leverage your skills and talents for career advancement. Seek out projects, initiatives, or roles that align with your expertise and allow you to showcase your abilities.

Continuously Develop and Evolve: Invest in ongoing learning and development to enhance your skills and stay relevant in your field. Seek out training programs, workshops, or certifications that can expand your knowledge and capabilities. Stay updated on industry trends and emerging technologies that could offer new avenues for leveraging your skills.

Remember always that, leveraging your skills and talents is an ongoing process. It requires self-awareness, adaptability, and a growth mindset. By continuously refining and expanding your skills, connecting with the right opportunities and people, and positioning yourself as a valuable resource, you can maximize your earning potential and create a fulfilling career or business based on your unique abilities.

www.ingramcontent.com/pod-product-compliance
Lightning Source LLC
LaVergne TN
LVHW010226070526
838199LV00062B/4736